simply romantic®

tips to

ROMANCE

your wife

Foreword by Dennis Rainey

FamilyLife Publishing®
Little Rock, Arkansas

Tips to Romance Your Wife
FamilyLife Publishing®
5800 Ranch Drive
Little Rock, Arkansas 72223
1-800-FL-TODAY • FamilyLife.com
FLTI, d/b/a FamilyLife®, is a ministry of Campus Crusade for Christ International®

ISBN: 978-1-60200-710-9

Printed in the United States of America

Second Edition

20 19 18 17 16   1 2 3 4 5

FAMILYLIFE®

CONTENTS

Foreword by Dennis Rainey   v

Tips to Romance Your Wife

Romantic Messages   1

Romantic Touch   17

Romantic Gifts   29

Romantic Moments   45

Romantic Moves   61

Romantic Advice   77

Romantic Holidays & Special Days   93

Appendix   104

FOREWORD

Most men need some inspiration to spark romance—Simply Romantic® *Tips to Romance Your Wife* is packed with inspiring ideas to help ordinary guys express love in extraordinary ways.

Barbara likes to remember the time when I surprised her with a trip to New England. Although that particular event took a lot of planning, expressing love can be as easy as tucking a short note inside her favorite magazine.

May I encourage you to take time to show your sweetheart that you care. By using this little book to affirm your love, she will be encouraged . . . your friendship will deepen . . . and romance will be sparked.

Dennis Rainey

Dennis Rainey
President and CEO of FamilyLife®
Father of six and grandfather of numerous grandchildren

ROMANTIC MESSAGES

1

Give your wife a small journal for recording her
secret romantic wishes. Read it regularly . . .
and then make her wishes come true.

Using dry-erase markers,
leave a note to your sweetie on the
bathroom mirror.

Using Post-it notes all around the house,
list the reasons why you love your wife.
Hide some of them in places where
it might take days for her to find.

Make a play list of some of her romantic songs and save it on her phone or computer. Include a love message that you record for her.

Call your wife on the phone and,
in a whisper, tell her all of the places you'd like
to kiss her the next time you see her.

Send your sweetie a subtle,
but suggestive, e-mail or
text message.

The next time you and your
wife have to be apart,
leave a note for her to
open each day.

Sneak a note into her
vehicle that reads, "You have me all revved up!
Put the car in gear and race on
over to (location)."

Write out your wedding vows on a small
card and sign your name to them.
Put the card somewhere where
she will see it every day.

Make a list of all the things your sweetheart
does for you that you probably take for
granted. Thank her for each one.

11

Compliment your wife in front of others—
especially your kids. You may be the only
one in her life who's doing it!

Tuck a note inside your wife's cosmetic
bag or near her hairbrush for her to find
when she gets ready in the morning.

Send your wife an invitation to a night of romance. Have the envelope postmarked from Romance, Arkansas 72136.

Scour the Internet for the perfect
romantic e-card. Send it to your wife
when she least expects it.

15

Tell your wife you love her every
morning and every night.

ROMANTIC TOUCH

16

Pamper her with a pedicure—administered
by you. You will need a basin of warm water
with bubbles, some candles, and a pedicure set
(available at most discount stores).

Celebrate Bubble Bath Night once a
month with your wife. Light candles,
prepare a bath, warm a towel, serve her
favorite beverage, and then wash her.

18

Hold her hand whenever you are in public together.

19

Caress her hands as you give her a hand
massage. Express appreciation for the
various things she does with hands that
show love and care for others.

Sign up as a couple for dancing lessons—
let her choose the style: ballroom, swing,
square dance, etc.

21

A woman's ears are very sensitive.
Spend time nuzzling her neck and ears.

Play the "Touching Game." Make 10 cards
describing "Ways to Touch," and 10 cards
with "Places to Touch" (one idea per card).
Without looking, pull one card from each
pile and then take action!

23

Play footsie with her the next time
you are having dinner with your in-laws.

24

Snuggle (just snuggle!) in bed and tell her
all the things you admire about her.

25

The next time you're sitting with
your wife in church, reach out and
put your arm around her.

26

When you see your wife after work, kiss her.
Not just a peck on the cheek. *Really* kiss her.

27

Make foreplay the focus. Take your time.
Focus on her: Play with her hair, caress her
face, and gently stroke her arms and legs.
Let things build slowly.

ROMANTIC GIFTS

28

Make a stop on your way home
from work and pick up that special
treat your wife loves.

29

Leave one of your wife's dress shoes in the
front seat of the car. Tuck a note inside,
telling her that she is your Cinderella
and that she is to meet you at a certain
time and place so you can buy her
a new pair of shoes.

30

Plan a romantic weekend at a
bed-and-breakfast. Make all of the
arrangements yourself.

31

Start filling up a jar with your loose change.
Let your wife know that when the jar is
full, you will redeem the change for a gift
card from her favorite store.

32

Ask your wife, "What can I do to help you today?" Allow her to share a worry or a situation where she needs a helping hand or prayer.

33

Surprise her with an unexpected gift.
It doesn't have to be expensive—
just something to let her know you
were thinking of her.

34

If your wife is a collector of figurines, tea cups, etc., buy her something that adds to her collection.

Take $10 to the Dollar Store and buy her
10 fun gifts that remind you of her. Over
dinner, give them to her one at a time and
tell her why you bought each item.

36

Let her purchase what she considers
sexy pajamas. Plan a special night for
the fashion show.

37

When your wife comments on something
she would really like to have, make a note of
it and purchase it for her at Christmas
(see appendix).

38

Wrap up a skeleton key in a box
with a note that says,
"You hold the key to my heart."

Secretly buy her tickets to a special event
(concert, game, exhibit). Plan a lunch or
dinner date on the day of the event.
After dessert, give her the tickets.

Present her with a special piece of jewelry.
Make it even more personal by having a
message engraved.

Get tickets for two (and that includes you)
to a "chick flick" she wants to see.

Play "Let's Make a Deal." Buy her three
gifts and wrap them separately. Let her
choose which one to open. Have fun
trying to change her mind. Put the
other two away for later.

ROMANTIC MOMENTS

43

Create your own romantic drive-in
movie experience. Drive to a remote location. Set
up a portable DVD player or streaming device in
the front seat of the car while you and your wife
snuggle in the backseat enjoying the
snacks you brought along.

Turn your bedroom into a romantic getaway:
rose petals, scented candles, and soft music.
Then romance your lover.

45

Remember how much you talked when you were dating? How polite you were? Try that for one week and watch what happens.

46

Feed your wife chocolate-covered strawberries that you made yourself. Wash and dry the strawberries and dip them in melted chocolate chips.

47

Remember what makes your wife laugh
and then tickle her "funny bone." Laughter
makes any day better.

Rent a convertible one weekend
just for the fun of it.
Drive her to her favorite places.

49

Enjoy a second, third, or fourth honeymoon. Make reservations to spend the night at a nice hotel in your area. If money is tight, start saving $5 or $10 per week until you have enough.

Circle a day on the calendar and take your
wife on a mystery date. As the day gets
closer leave her clues: what to wear, when
to be ready, etc. Keep it a surprise.

51

Over coffee ask your wife, "What are the three
most romantic times we've had together?"
Remember what they are and make
plans to do them again.

Bathe the kids. Clean the kitchen.
Fold the laundry. Make the bed.
Do whatever it is she normally does.
Tell her to relax.

53

It's Christmas in July—hang a stocking
with a lacy garter belt and fill it with
goodies (e.g., whipped cream, chocolate
syrup). Offer yourself as a tasty treat.

Find the book your wife is reading and
leave some encouraging notes in
it every 20 pages or so.

55

Take her on a date to a bookstore.
Tell her you'd like to find a book you can
read together. Suggestion: *Rekindling the
Romance* by Dennis and Barbara Rainey
(available at ShopFamilyLife.com).

56

Do something together: Take a class, play tennis, start a walking program, remodel a room, or plant a vegetable garden. Just do it together.

What kinds of games does your wife like to
play? Cards? Board games? Sports?
Play her favorite one.

Late one night grab a blanket and your wife and head outdoors. Find a nice spot to lie back and look at the stars together.

ROMANTIC MOVES

59

Arrange for a babysitter and then whisk
your wife away for a special day filled
with fun things she enjoys.

On those chilly mornings go
out and warm up her car.
Now *that's* romantic!

61

Take an afternoon off and catch a
matinee. Sit in the back row.

62

You probably already know,
but find out your lover's
least favorite chore—and then
do it for her for a month.

63

When you are away from your wife
during the day, send her a text message
or short e-mail letting her know you are
praying for her and looking forward to
being with her that evening.

Tell your wife you'd like to start
exercising together so that you'll
both be around to enjoy each
other longer.

65

Ask her what she enjoys in bed.
Do it regularly.

66

Develop a special sign or
secret word just for her that
communicates your love.

67

Fantasize about your wife, and then
tell her what you were thinking.

68

Take some time out of your busy
schedule to cook your wife a meal.
Serve the meal by candlelight using
your wedding china.

69

Leave roses in the front seat of
her vehicle—just because.

Put your wife to bed . . . tuck
her in . . . tell her a story
(make it a romantic story).

Wash her car. Be sure
to vacuum it, too.

Treat your wife to a horse-drawn
carriage ride.

73

Get into the habit of buying her
silly souvenirs when you're out
on a date. Purchase (or make) a
special box where she can store
her keepsakes.

ROMANTIC ADVICE

74

It takes your wife's body longer
than yours to become aroused—
so don't skip the foreplay.

Practice good hygiene. Brush your teeth,
take a shower, and put on clean clothes
before you romance your sweetie.

76

Remain faithful to your wife in your heart,
in your mind, and in your actions.

Good manners and chivalry are romantic.

78

Be a student of your spouse. Find out
what she likes and dislikes, her strengths
and weaknesses, and her fears.

79

Women view romance differently from men.
Ask your wife to describe what's romantic to her.
Don't be surprised when her ideas
sound very different from yours.

Remember your wife is God's gift to *you*.
Thank Him for her, then tell her you did so.

81

Plan a vacation together—in ink.

Look in her eyes and just listen.

83

Arrange a date with your wife at least once
a month. Mark it on your calendar and take
the initiative to make it happen!

Tell her you would marry her
all over again.

85

Ask your wife to write down three things she'd like you to start doing, three things she'd like you to stop doing, and three things she'd like you to keep doing. Read the list and do it.

The next time your favorite team (or show)
is on TV, skip it and take her shopping or
out to dinner. Let her know that she is more
important than what you're giving up.

87

To strengthen your marriage, make
plans to attend a Weekend to Remember®
marriage getaway. For a schedule of
events visit FamilyLife.com/Weekend.

88

Write down anniversaries, special days,
sizes, etc. (see appendix).

89

Be resolute in romancing your love
all year long. Choose your favorite ideas
from this little book and enter them
into your phone or digital calendar
January through December.

On Valentine's Day, stage a progressive dinner
and serve each course in a different room.
End the evening with dessert in the bedroom!

91

March 17 is St. Patrick's Day. Celebrate it by leaving your wife a note that says, "I'm lucky to have you by my side."

Make memories on Memorial Day.
Use your phone or digital camera to take
snapshots of you and your spouse together.
You might need to ask others to
take the pictures.

93

Celebrate summer by taking advantage of the
longest day of the year. Start with breakfast in
bed, treat her to lunch, then end the day with a
summertime barbecue for two.

94

This Fourth of July, light up your own fireworks in the night sky. Add glow-in-the-dark stars to your bedroom ceiling—and snuggle under your own private starry sky.

Each day in the month of August leave her a
Hershey's kiss where she'll be sure to find it. Ask
her to save the paper flags in a jar and redeem
them for actual kisses.

As the days begin to turn chilly, take your "pumpkin" to the pumpkin patch. Let her choose a few to accent your front door. Bring along a thermos of hot apple cider to share.

97

On the third Saturday in October buy your
sweetheart a few fall treats for Sweetest Day:
popcorn balls, caramel apples, and candy
corn, to name a few.

98

Don't be a turkey this Thanksgiving—help
your wife in the kitchen! And don't forget
to tell her why you're thankful for her.

99

On Christmas Eve give your
"Mrs. Claus" a basket full of bubble
bath supplies and then get the
water ready for her.

APPENDIX

Sizes for Her:

Jeans: _____

Slacks: _____

Shirt: _____

Shoes: _____

Ring: _____

Other: _____

_____

GIFT LIST

_____

_____

_____

_____

_____

_____

_____